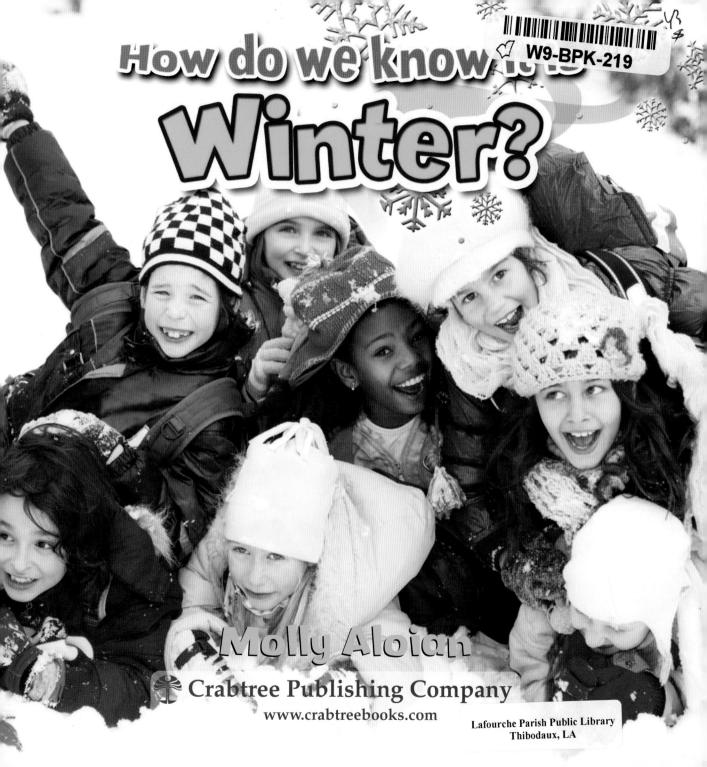

How do we know it is Winter?

Molly Aloian

Crabtree Publishing Company

www.crabtreebooks.com

Dedicated by Samara Parent
Happy 4th Birthday Georgina! xoxo

Author
Molly Aloian

Publishing plan research and development
Sean Charlebois, Reagan Miller
Crabtree Publishing Company

Editorial director
Kathy Middleton

Editors
Adrianna Morganelli
Crystal Sikkens

Design
Samara Parent
Margaret Amy Salter

Photo research
Samara Parent

Production coordinator
and prepress technician
Margaret Amy Salter

Print coordinator
Katherine Berti

Illustrations
Katherine Berti: page 6

Photographs
iStockPhoto: page 1
Thinkstock: pages 4 (fall), 19 (top)
All other images by Shutterstock

Library and Archives Canada Cataloguing in Publication

Aloian, Molly
    How do we know it is winter? / Molly Aloian.

(Seasons close-up)
Includes index.
Issued also in electronic formats.
ISBN 978-0-7787-0962-6 (bound).--ISBN 978-0-7787-0966-4 (pbk.)

    1. Winter--Juvenile literature. 2. Seasons--Juvenile literature.
I. Title. II. Series: Seasons close-up

QB637.8.A56 2013   j508.2   C2012-907340-7

Library of Congress Cataloging-in-Publication Data

CIP available at Library of Congress

Crabtree Publishing Company

www.crabtreebooks.com   1-800-387-7650

Printed in Hong Kong/012013/BK20121102

Published in Canada
Crabtree Publishing
616 Welland Ave.
St. Catharines, Ontario
L2M 5V6

Published in the United States
Crabtree Publishing
PMB 59051
350 Fifth Avenue, 59th Floor
New York, New York 10118

Published in the United Kingdom
Crabtree Publishing
Maritime House
Basin Road North, Hove
BN41 1WR

Published in Australia
Crabtree Publishing
3 Charles Street
Coburg North
VIC 3058

Contents

What is winter?

Winter is the coldest **season** of the year. It always comes after fall and before spring. Every year, spring changes into summer and summer changes into fall. Fall turns into winter and winter turns back to spring.

What do you think?

Do you notice a pattern, or cycle, to the seasons?

Spring

Summer

Fall

Winter

Cold outside

During winter, the weather is cold and snow falls on the ground. People usually spend more time inside. When people go outside, they must wear warm clothes, such as jackets, hats, and scarves. What do you wear when you go outside during winter?

The Sun still shines in winter, but the air is very cold.

Why do we have winter?

Every year Earth takes 12 months to circle around the Sun. As its moving around the Sun, Earth spins on a tilted **axis**, or imaginary line. This causes different parts of Earth to get more sunlight at different times of the year. The different amounts of sunlight gives us our seasons.

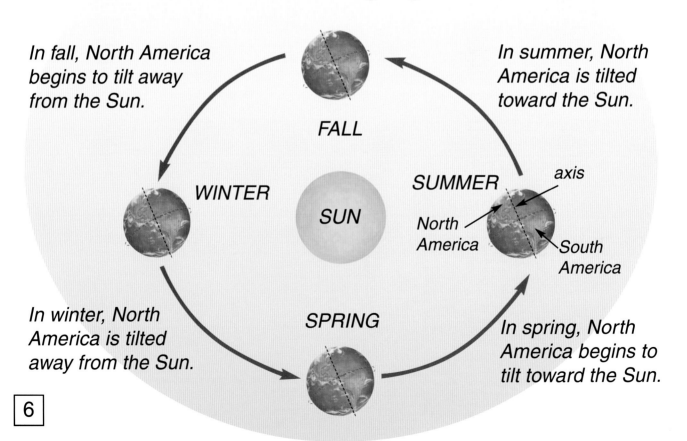

In fall, North America begins to tilt away from the Sun.

In summer, North America is tilted toward the Sun.

FALL

SUMMER

axis

WINTER

SUN

North America

South America

In winter, North America is tilted away from the Sun.

SPRING

In spring, North America begins to tilt toward the Sun.

Tilted away

During winter in North America, the northern parts of Earth are tilted away from the Sun. This means the days have less sunlight and cold temperatures. The southern parts of Earth are tilted toward the Sun. This means they are getting summer with hot temperatures and longer days.

What do you think?

Cold winds and falling snow are signs that winter has arrived. What are some other signs of winter?

When is winter?

In North America, the first day of winter is in December. Winter, like the other seasons, lasts for about three months. During winter, the Sun rises late and sets early, so the days are short. Long, dark, cold nights are signs that winter has arrived.

You can still have fun at night in winter. The white snow often makes it brighter.

Different times

In some parts of the world, there are only two seasons—the wet season and the dry season. During the wet season, there is heavy rain. During the dry season, there is very little rain.

These elephants are looking for water during the dry season in Africa.

Winter weather

In winter, the weather is cold. Snowflakes or **sleet** fall on the ground. Snowflakes form when water in clouds freezes into **ice crystals**. Cold winds sometimes blow snow into huge **snowdrifts**.

What do you think?

What three things do you like about winter? What three things do you dislike about winter?

Winter blizzards

There are sometimes **blizzards** in winter. Blizzards are snowstorms with strong winds and very cold temperatures. Heavy snow can block driveways and roads. Roads can become icy. Schools, offices, and businesses sometimes close during blizzards because heavy snow and icy roads make traveling difficult.

snowdrift

Plants in winter

Plants pass the winter in different ways. Trees lose their leaves and flowers **wither** and die. Some plants store food in their roots, stems, and leaves, and become **dormant** during winter. These plants can use the stored food to begin growing again in spring.

Being green

Evergreen trees do not lose their leaves. They stay green all winter. They have tough, waxy, narrow leaves called needles. Many bushes and trees have thick bark that protects them from the cold and prevents them from drying out.

Animals in winter

These snow geese are gathering to fly to a warmer place for the winter.

Some animals, such as certain birds, **migrate**, or move to a warmer place, before winter begins. Other animals, such as chipmunks, **hibernate** during winter. They crawl into underground holes or nests and sleep through the coldest part of winter.

Fur coats

Animals that do not migrate or hibernate have thick coats of fur to keep them warm. Beavers, foxes, and rabbits all have thick fur. Snowshoe hares have white fur. Having white fur helps them hide from **predators** in the snow.

What do you think?

Can you think of three other animals that you see in winter that have thick fur to keep them warm.

Beaver

Fox

Snowshoe Hare

15

Winter fun

There are plenty of fun things to do in winter. People dress in warm clothes so they can go outside and play in the snow. Many people go sledding in winter. Some people make snowmen or snow angels. Other people ice skate, ski, or ice fish in winter.

This girl has built a snowman as tall as her!

What do you think?

Can you think what winter clothes have in common?

Winter wear

People stay warm outside by wearing layers of clothes. People wear winter jackets, snow pants, hats, scarves, and gloves or mittens. Thick socks and winter boots help keep our feet warm and dry.

Winter foods

In winter, people often eat warm foods. For breakfast, many people eat bowls of hot oatmeal. Some people put nuts or fruit on top of their oatmeal. Eating a hot breakfast is a good way to start a winter day.

What do you think?

What are some of your favorite winter foods?

This boy is enjoying a hot bowl of oatmeal on a cold winter day.

Soups and stews

After spending the day outside in the cold, many people eat steaming bowls of soups and stews with meat and vegetables. Drinking hot chocolate is another way to warm up in winter.

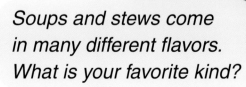

Soups and stews come in many different flavors. What is your favorite kind?

Moving snow

In winter, keeping highways, streets, and sidewalks clear is an important job. Huge snowplows clear the snow off of highways and streets. People use snowblowers or shovels to remove snow from sidewalks and driveways.

Snowblowers are machines that pick up snow and blow it to a new area.

Salt trucks are often seen after a light snowfall or when the roads are icy.

Spreading salt

Special trucks spread salt on streets and highways in winter. The salt helps melt the snow and ice. The streets and highways are less slippery when snow and ice are melted. They are safer for cars, trucks, and other vehicles.

What do you think?

Clearing snow helps us stay safe during winter. What other ways do we prepare for cold, snowy weather?

Winter around the world

We know what winter is like in North America. What is winter like in other places around the world? This activity will help you discover what winter is like in Sydney, Australia. Use books and the Internet to find out what winter is like in Sydney. Try to answer the following questions:

When does winter begin in Sydney, Australia?

How long does winter last?

What kind of clothing would you need to pack if you were visiting Sydney in winter?

What are three popular winter activities in Sydney, Australia?

Learning more

Books

The Story of Snow: The Science of Winter's Wonder by Mark Cassino.
Chronicle Books, 2009.

What Is Weather? (Weather Close-Up) by Robin Johnson.
Crabtree Publishing Company, 2012.

Which Season Is It? (My World) by Bobbie Kalman.
Crabtree Publishing Company, 2011.

Winter (Four Seasons) by Nuria Roca. Barron's Educational Series, 2004.

Websites

Changing Seasons – Exploring Nature Educational Resource
www.exploringnature.org/db/detail.php?dbID=112&detID=2634

Earth's Seasons – Zoom Astronomy
www.enchantedlearning.com/subjects/astronomy/planets/earth/Seasons.shtml

Science projects: ideas, topics, methods, and examples
www.sciencemadesimple.com/

Seasons – Science for Kids!
www.historyforkids.org/scienceforkids/physics/weather/seasons.htm

Words to know

axis (AK-sis) noun The straight line around which Earth rotates

blizzard (BLIZ-erd) noun A snowstorm with strong winds and cold temperatures

dormant (DAWR-muhnt) adjective Not active or growing

hibernate (HI-ber-neyt) verb To go through winter in a sleeping or resting state

ice crystals (ahys KRIS-tls) noun Tiny pieces of ice

migrate (MAHY-greyt) verb Moving from one place to another for warmer weather or food

predator (PRED-uh-ter) noun An animal that hunts and eats other animals

season (SEE-zuhn) noun A period of time with certain temperatures and weather

sleet (SLEET) noun Frozen or partly frozen rain

snowdrift (SNOH-drift) noun A bank or hill of snow

wither (WITH-er) verb To shrivel and dry out

A *noun* is a person, place, or thing. A *verb* is an action word that tells you what someone or something does. An *adjective* is a word that tells you what something is like.

Index

24